Toasts to the Bride
and
How to Propose Them

Toasts to the Bride

and
How to Propose Them

BY

MERVYN J. HUSTON

HURTIG

Publishers

EDMONTON

This book is dedicated to Barbara

Copyright © 1968 by Mervyn J. Huston

First printing 1968
Tenth printing 1984

Hurtig Publishers
10560 105 Street
Edmonton, Alberta

ISBN 0-88830-007-7

Printed and bound in Canada
by John Deyell Company

Contents

Preface

So you have been asked to propose the Toast to the Bride! You have been paid a great compliment. Of all of the friends of the bride and her family you have been the one chosen to make the most important address of the occasion. It is up to you to do a good job of it. This will require considerable thought, care, and preparation but if you follow the principles set out in this book you can be assured of success and can make an important contribution to the enjoyment of a delightful affair.

In giving a toast to the bride you have a good many factors working in your favor. Your remarks will take only a few minutes; you will never have a more receptive audience; everyone is happy and relaxed and responsive; they are all on your side and pulling for you; all you have to do is to put into a few words the good wishes of the assembly. However, do not be misled by this deceptive simplicity. You have an important responsibility and only a few minutes to discharge it. If you do not express the sentiments of the audience you have failed your duty. The secret is very simple; be like a good Boy Scout—*Be Prepared.*

I shall assume that you are not a skilled and experienced speaker. If you are, there is no harm done and you can get some useful tips for this specific assignment. The format of this book is as follows: general comments on good public speaking; application of these principles to a toast to the bride; a list of appropriate quotations and epigrams; examples of toasts; and suggestions concerning the response by the bridegroom.

The best way to use this book is to read it through first. Do not leap immediately to a part that interests you. After you have read the book return to those parts you have marked as being pertinent for you. Browse around and select bits and pieces in the preparation of your own toast. The examples of toasts have been included as prototypes and you may not wish to use any one per se. They will serve to show how the principles can be applied, and ideas and parts may be adapted to your own use.

 *Acknowledgments*

 wish to thank the Reverend E. J. White for advice in the preparation of this book and Tony Cashman for reading the manuscript and for his helpful suggestions.

I
General Principles

TOAST to the bride must subscribe to all the tenets of good public speaking. All the factors involved in the preparation and delivery of an effective speech are applicable to the presentation of a toast. This chapter summarizes the general principles involved in effective speaking. Chapter II deals with the toast itself.

PREPARATION

Think. Give yourself lots of time. Let ideas float around in your mind for days. Read. Look up references, quotations, epigrams, essays, etc. Make copious notes. Ideas have a distressing way of floating away if they are not written down. Carry a card with you at all times and jot down ideas, phrases, bons mots, stories.

Organize. The next step is to organize this accumulated material into a systematic sequence. Organize and reorganize. Write an outline. Ruthlessly discard extraneous or inappropriate material even if you like it. In the earlier stages include more material than you can use. It is easier to eliminate than to add. Then boil it down to a length suitable to the time you will have.

Write. Write out your entire speech word for word as you would plan to give it. You won't give it this way but it will help to organize your thoughts and facilitate your language. Strive for simplicity in language. Be yourself. Use ordinary words but avoid slang or colloquialisms except for effect. Look up in a dictionary the meaning and pronunciation of any word of more than one syllable. People are frightfully snobbish about words and you can ruin your effect by a mistake. Do not be pedantic, affected, or pretentious or you will lay the biggest egg since the roc. Rewrite and polish. Add and subtract. Rewrite and polish.

Abstract. When you have your speech in reasonable shape put it in a format for delivery. Do this on cards. Paper has a distressing habit of fluttering in nervous hands. Write out the first two sentences in full. This will get you launched even if you are nervous and suffering a bit from stage fright. Once you get started you will gain confidence and be okay. Thereafter on your cards write headings, cue words, punch lines, or underline these. In a short speech such as a toast it is usually satisfactory to write the text out in full and underline. Write quotations out in full. Write large so the words can be read easily at the distance you will be using when speaking. Number the cards in sequence.

Rehearse. Do not memorize your speech. But read it over and over again until you virtually know it by heart. Read at first silently until you know it well, and then aloud. You will find parts you don't like the sound of. Polish and improve. Then try giving your speech using the Abstract. Practice standing in front of the mirror. Speak slowly. Check your stance, expressiveness, emphasis, movement, gestures, facial expression, and voice modulation. Your eyes should be up and away from the text at least 95% of the time.

Experiment. You may feel a little foolish doing this but it is better to feel foolish in solitude than to appear foolish in public. Experiment with ad lib comments. Time your speech. Bring in members of your family or friends and listen, with reservations, to their suggestions. This will be a tougher audience than you will ever meet in public, believe me. If you can gain access to the hall or place where you are to speak, try out your talk there.

Humor. Humor is a useful weapon in public speaking but a dangerous one. You may cut your own thumb on it—if not your throat. Don't try to be funny if you have no talent for humor—be honest with yourself. Stories and anecdotes are useful to relax and amuse your audience and may be used if they make a point pertinent to your subject and are appropriate to the occasion. Remember a blue note is a sour note. Don't laugh at your own jokes—you may be laughing alone. Unless you are a skillful raconteur (which is unlikely) do not undertake dialect stories. Do not use any witticism which takes longer than twenty-six seconds. Do not introduce a story with such hackneyed comments as: "I understand I should open with a story," or "That reminds me of a story - -" etc. Just tell it. Quotations, epigrams, and quips are, in general, safer than stories.

PRESENTATION

Now that your talk has been thoroughly prepared, written, and rehearsed, let us consider the factors that will make for a good presentation.

Preliminaries. While you are being introduced take several deep breaths. This will reduce the breathlessness common at the beginning of a speech. Be near at hand—not at the back of the room. Walk unhurriedly to the lectern, podium, or microphone. Do not begin right away. Pause and look out at the audience for a count of ten. This will give them a chance to shuffle their chairs, get comfortable, and focus their attention on you. It will also give you a chance to collect your wits.

The Opening. Always address the Chair. You may also include distinguished personages if you wish but this has its hazards. You may overlook someone who thinks he should be mentioned and if your list becomes long it becomes absurd. The safest thing is to begin simply: "Mr. Chairman (pause). Ladies and Gentlemen (long pause). In the words of that great philosopher Confucius—(pause)." Now you are launched. You may thank your introducer if you wish but it is not essential. Listen to your introduction and you may find some comment you can turn to your advantage. If nothing bright occurs to you, forget it.

Posture. Stand relaxed but don't lean or droop. Stand still, but not stiff. Don't jitter, tap-dance, or shuffle around. Keep one hand for your notes. The other you can put briefly in your coat pocket with the thumb out, and the rest of the time just let it hang. Use gestures if they are natural. Don't fuss with cutlery, plates, or bread crumbs.

The Mike. If there is a microphone use it, but don't fiddle with it, move it, or refer to it. If at all possible try to test it beforehand. If not, note the experience of previous speakers and govern yourself accordingly. In general a distance of about a foot is right. Don't shout—the function of the P.A. system is to make this unnecessary. Use a normal voice volume. Don't lean toward it, and if you need to cough or clear your throat turn your head away. You must keep the distance from mouth to mike fairly constant so that you don't fade out as you turn away and zoom in when you turn back. Your voice may sound strange to you if you have not used a P.A. before so don't be alarmed if you don't recognize yourself.

Voice. If you do not have a P.A. system, then *speak up*. More speeches are ruined because they can't be heard than by any other cause. Keep the pitch low but the volume up. Don't shout, but it is better to be too loud than too soft. Don't be a monotone —vary pitch and rhythm but not so much as to be artificial or oratorical. Breath deeply from the abdomen. Enunciate and articulate carefully. Watch those terminal "g's" on words like "going"; and be sure "Ladies and Gentlemen" doesn't come out, "Laze and Gem." Don't intersperse your comments with meaningless sounds like "duh," "ah," "uh," "er," etc.

Speed. The speed of delivery should be slightly slower than conversation. Start your speech slowly and speed up later when you have the attention of the audience. About 100 to 150 words per minute is reasonable. Use more pauses than in conversation. Pause at the end of sentences and longer after a paragraph. Pause for emphasis before and after punch lines. Don't kill applause or laughter—give them lots of time.

Nerves. So you're nervous! So what! Every good speaker, *no matter how experienced,* is excited when making a speech. That's all nerves are—excitement. And you should be excited or you won't do a good job. There is no antibiotic to cure you of nervousness. Just accept it and use it to your advantage. Thorough preparation will give you the confidence which will minimize nervousness. You may be nervous but no one else needs to know it. Never refer to the fact that you are nervous. Make no mention of knocking knees, butterflies in the stomach, or sweaty hands. Never denigrate yourself. It's either false modesty or you have no business up there on the podium. Your voice may wobble a bit but it will be more noticeable to you than to others. Ignore it. Don't correct simple errors in words or smile or shake your head or whistle if you bobble a word. Don't magnify self-consciousness or inconsequential errors.

II
The Toast

YOU are now ready to apply the general principles previously described to the formulation of a toast to the bride. All of the instructions concerning preparation, rehearsal, and presentation are applicable.

PREPARATION

Purpose. A toast is a tribute. It is your function to pay a tribute to the bride and to express the good wishes of the assembly. It is now general custom to include the bridegroom in the remarks and to wish happiness to the couple.

Length. Be brief. Most toasts to the bride are too long. This is because the speaker knows he has an important job to do and he goes all out. A long toast defeats its purpose, bores the audience, and embarrasses the bride. Don't be longer than four minutes. Check this out in your rehearsals.

Humor. It is neither necessary nor desirable to keep them rolling in the aisles. Your task is a serious one but it should be lightened with some appropriate drollery. Stories are useful if appropriate. If you use one, don't be longer than twenty-six seconds. Quotations, epigrams, and anecdotes are also helpful. Don't be smutty—no reference to shotguns, sex, beds, pills, or rabbits. If you are in any doubt at all about the propriety of a remark, leave it out. Comments about mothers-in-law, money, honeymoons, race, and liquor are fraught with peril. You may mention the bride's popularity but don't make reference to any beau in particular—the bridegroom may be jealous. Do not say anything that will embarrass the bride, her family, the bridegroom, or anyone there.

Content. The person chosen to give the toast to the bride is usually, and preferably, an older person so that he may bring maturity, judgment, and dignity to his comments. If the proposer is approximately the same age as the bride and groom, it would be impertinent and unwise to indulge in sage advice or pontifical profundities. If such is the case, confine yourself to the charm and beauty of the bride, the good fortune of the groom, facetious comment, and advice and best wishes. (See Examples #6, 9, 10, 15, 16, 17.)

The content of your talk depends entirely on you. There is no set format. Let your comments reflect your own distinctive personality. If you are serious minded let your talk be serious; if you are jovial let the humor shine through. Be yourself.

You may rely on your own ideas and wit or you may use quotations—or preferably both. This book is predicated on the assumption that you are not a potent and original wit and are looking for ideas and quotable phrases. Chapter III contains a substantial number of usable quotes from which you can select or adapt. This list is derived from poets, writers, and others; some are my own; and some are of unknown source or general conversational coin. (If I have missed the author of certain phrases, my apologies—I have tried to give all devils their due.) Chapter IV demonstrates how these ideas and quotations can be woven into a talk. It has been said that quotation is a crutch for a feeble wit—but it is better to use a crutch than to fall on your face.

I shall set out certain themes that may be used. One of these ideas may form the basis of your talk or several may be combined or interwoven.

(i) EULOGY ON THE BRIDE. This is a good approach if not overdone, since a toast is a tribute. You should be flattering but not fulsome or you will embarrass her. You are probably an old friend of the family and have known the bride for many years. You may begin with some reminiscences that lend themselves to kindly humor. It's all right to be a little sentimental but don't be maudlin. Do not indulge in an exhaustive biography that traces her life interminably from the time she was in rompers. Emphasize those qualities in her which will make her a successful wife. Putting the shot is not one of these (see Example #2).

(ii) RELIGIOUS, PHILOSOPHICAL, OR MORAL THEMES. Your talk may be entirely serious or preferably may have touches of humor. Choose one basic idea (or a few) based on quotation and develop it; or you may use such themes as part of your talk. Don't try to cover too much ground and don't preach a sermon. (Most of the Examples use such themes.)

(iii) ADVICE. You may indulge in a little serious and humorous advice on how to adjust to the married state and how to meet the challenges of the future. (See Examples #4 and 12.)

(iv) BEST WISHES. You may elaborate on the nature of the hopes and wishes you have for the couple. (See Example #3.)

(v) LOVE. Love is the basis of marriage and you may discuss the nature of love and how love serves to join a couple together in holy wedlock. The beautiful passage in First Corinthians, 13, is applicable here and frequently forms part of the wedding ceremony. (See Examples #2 and 5.)

(vi) SPECIAL INTERESTS. If you know of some special interest or activity or enthusiasm of one or both of the partners you can make use of this, usually facetiously. For example: tennis (love match); skiing (sitz marks in the snows of time); music (see Example #6); fishing (hook, line, and sinker); bridge (grand slam; doubled and vulnerable); stamp collecting; boating, or swimming (sea of matrimony); baseball (home run; out in center field); ice hockey and football (see Example #10).

(vii) VOCATION. You can work in references to the vocations of either or of both bride and bridegroom. Show how this training can be applied to marriage or draw parallels between these vocations and marriage. This is usually facetious. (See Example #10.) Some vocations, together with some quotations and clues are listed on the following pages.

Banker Bankers are just like anybody else, except richer. (Ogden Nash)

Beautician To paint the lily, to throw a perfume on the violet. (Shakespeare)

Beauty's but skin deep. (John Davies)

Businessman Business is business. (F. P. Adams)

The maxim of the British people is "Business as usual." (Winston Churchill)

Dentist The only man who can with impunity tell a woman to close her mouth.

I am glad that my Adonis hath a sweete tooth in his head. (John Lyly)

There was never yet philosopher that could endure the toothache patiently. (Shakespeare)

Doctor An apple a day keeps the doctor away. (Anonymous)

Doctors is all swabs. (R. L. Stevenson in *Treasure Island*)

Deceive not thy physician. (G. Herbert)

Engineer Anyone who can use a slide rule—this is called rule of thumb.

Beware of engineers—remember the most famous of them all was Casey Jones, and he is noted for a foul up and his brother struck out.

Executive If a man has an office with a desk on which there is a buzzer, and if he can press that buzzer and have somebody come dashing in response—then he's an executive. (E. F. Andrews)

An executive at the office and a clerk at home.

Farmer Has the real dirt, but not the low down.

The farmers . . . are the founders of human civilization. (Webster)

When the sun shineth, make hay. (Heywood, 1497-1580)

Lawyer A married lawyer is a legal eagle with his claws clipped.

"If the law supposes that," said Mr. Bumble, "the law is a ass, a idiot." (Charles Dickens)

Newspaperman Spends a lot of time writing stuff to wrap to-morrow's garbage in.

Nurse He took a turn for the nurse. (Common saying)
When pain and anguish wring the brow,
A ministering angel thou! (Scott)

Pharmacist Has more solutions than problems.
An apothecary should never be out of spirits. (Sheridan)
When taken, to be well shaken. (George Colman, the Younger)

Policeman When constabulary duty's to be done, a policeman's lot is not an 'appy one. (Gilbert in *Pirates of Penzance*)

Politician I am not a politician and my other habits are good. (C. F. Browne)
Man is by nature a political animal. (Aristotle)
All politics is apple sauce. (Will Rogers)

Stenographer Will make a good wife; she is used to taking dictation.

Teacher And still the wonder grew, that one small head could carry all he (she) knew. (Goldsmith)

(viii) SATIRE. You may work in ironical comments or quotations by saying you don't believe them or you may give contradictory quotations. (See Examples #1 and 13.) Use satirical comments about marriage with caution if there is a history of marital difficulties in either family or you may get your finger in a woodpecker's nest.

(ix) SPECIAL THEMES. You may use similes, metaphors, analogies, allegories, fables, stories, or other special approaches. (See Example #11.) There is some danger in this as a theme since you may focus attention on your own cleverness and not on the bride. But such ideas may be worked in as part of another theme. Examples: drawing an analogy between marriage and a business concern or company; a steam engine, automobile, or other machine; an insurance policy; an orchestra; a football team; government; a ship on the sea of matrimony (this sea has largely been drained dry); a cup of wine (do not mention wine or liquor if the church disapproves of alcoholic beverages or if the bride's mother is president of the local temperance league). (See Examples #8, 9, 11, and 13.)

Second Marriage. If either the bride or groom has been married before, make no reference to it. This wedding marks a new era and the past is past. Choose your comments with particular care to avoid any possibility that they might be misconstrued in the light of past events.

PRESENTATION

Preamble. The toast to the bride may be given at the reception, at the rehearsal dinner, or at other times. It may be the only toast or there may be others, e.g. to the bridesmaids. The best man or other designate will be the master of ceremonies and will likely introduce you without elaboration other than as a friend of the bride or her family. Be on hand. Step forward to the appropriate place and wait for silence. Wedding affairs are usually noisy and gay, so allow adequate time for things to simmer down before beginning. If you do not get attention ask the chairman to call for quiet. Not until you have a reasonable amount of attention should you begin, but don't expect a deathlike hush.

The Bridegroom. In my research for this book I find that there is an increasing tendency to direct the comments of the toast to the couple rather than to the bride. The formal toast may be to the couple or to the bride. In any event be sure to make some comments about the groom—he is getting married also and should not be the forgotten man. You may recognize his good qualities or may tease him or play him off against his bride. Do not imply he is a clod, even if you think so. Today he is a prince. Don't overdo the part about how lucky he is. One instance reported to me concerned a proposer of the toast to the bride who, with well meaning fatuousness, extolled the virtues of the bride's family to such an extent and went on and on about how lucky the groom was to marry into such a wonderful family that everyone was very embarrassed. A later speaker trying to rectify the situation made matters worse. Another instance concerned a groom who had been pointedly ignored in the toast. When he gave his reply he thanked everyone even remotely connected with the ceremony including the janitor but not the proposer of the toast and received an ovation. If it is a mixed marriage, or if there are family rifts, feuds, reservations, or disappointments give no hint of such matters.

Opening. The usual opening is satisfactory. "Mr. Chairman (pause), Ladies and Gentlemen (pause)."

Speak Up. Many toasts to the bride are lost in the hubbub. If it is a sit-down affair or if you have a P.A. system, you will have little difficulty. However, if the reception is at a club or in a home with the guests milling about, you have a more difficult situation. Some magpies will continue to twitter so don't expect complete silence. Take a deep breath down into your abdomen and speak out as fully as you can without raising the pitch of your voice. Start slowly with several quite long pauses. Audience reaction is slow to build and slow to subside under such circumstances so give adequate time for response to any humorous sally. Don't wait too long, however, or you will lose attention.

Delivery. Keep eye contact with your audience as much as possible but turn toward the bride from time to time as you direct a remark her way. This will serve to focus attention upon the recipient of the toast.

The Formal Toast. When you have completed your remarks it is time to propose the formal toast. It is your function to direct and coordinate this part of the ceremony. Don't rush it. If the audience is seated, face them and say something to this effect: "And now, Ladies and Gentlemen, I shall ask you to rise." Give them adequate time to do so. If they are already standing, say: "I now ask you to raise your glasses." Then turning to the bride with your glass raised to her, say something like, "We wish you health and happiness in the years that lie ahead. To the Bride!" And you drink your toast. The audience will say, "To the Bride," and drink with you. You now fade into the background.

III
Quotations, Epigrams, and Quips

THE subjects which are most often referred to in a toast to the bride are marriage, love, women, wives, and husbands. Here are examples of what some other people have said on these subjects. You may incorporate these sayings in your talk, or better still, use them as a stimulus for your own imagination and as a guide to help you express ideas of your own.

MARRIAGE

It is not good that man should be alone. (*Genesis II, 18*)

Forsaking all others, keep thee only unto her, so long as ye both shall live. (*The Book of Common Prayer*)

With all my worldly goods I thee endow. (*English Book of Common Prayer*)

What therefore God hath joined together, let no man put asunder. (*Matthew XIX, 6*)

To have and to hold from this day forward, for better, for worse, for richer, for poorer, in sickness, and in health, to love and to cherish, till death do us part. (*The Book of Common Prayer*)

Can two walk together, except they be agreed. (*Amos III, 3*)

If a house be divided against itself, that house cannot stand. (*Mark III, 25*)

He that hath a wife and children hath given hostages to fortune; for they are impediments to great enterprises; either of virtue or mischief. (*Badon*)

I respect the institution of marriage. I have always thought that every woman should marry and no man. (*Disraeli*)

Keep your eyes open before marriage—half shut afterwards. (*Franklin*)

Loneliness is worse than unhappiness—that's the only excuse for marriage. (*M. J. H.*)

Men marry because they are tired, women because they are curious. Both are disappointed. (*Oscar Wilde*)

Marriage is a device of society designed to make trouble between two people who would otherwise get along very well. (*M. J. H.*)

Marriage is the only known example of the happy meeting of the immovable object and the irresistible force. (*Ogden Nash*)

A chap ought to save a few of the long evenings he spends with his girl till after they're married. (*Ken Hubbard*)

Marriage is the chalice that holds the wine of love. (*M. J. H.*)

The conception of two people living together for 25 years without having a cross word suggests a lack of spirit only to be admired in sheep. (*A. P. Herbert*)

Marriage is a good thing—no family should be without one. (*M. J. H.*)

The value of the marriage knot,
Contrary to popular thought,
Is not,
To give you a body to sleep with,
But to give you a soul to weep with. (*M. J. H.*)

'Tis safest in matrimony to begin with a little aversion. (Mrs. Malaprop in *The Rivals* by Sheridan)

Marriage—a community consisting of a master, a mistress, and two slaves, making in all, two. (*Bierce*)

A good marriage is that in which each appoints the other guardian of his solitude. (*Rilke*)

All comedies are ended by a marriage. (*Byron*)

Let there be spaces in your togetherness. (*Gibran*)

Marriage is not a mutual phagocytosis. (*M. J. H.*)

Marriage is a thing you've got to give your whole mind to. (*Ibsen*)

Marriage happens as with cages: the birds without despair to get in, and those within despair of getting out. (*Montaigne*)

Marriage is two fishes in the same net. (*M. J. H.*)

Marriage is fish and fisherman caught in the same net. (*M. J. H.*)

Marriage is a noose. (*Cervantes*)

Marriages are made in heaven. (*Tennyson*)

Marriage, if one will face the truth, is an evil, but a necessary evil. (*Menander, 343-292* B.C.)

Marriage is like life in this—that it is a field of battle, and not a bed of roses. (*R. L. Stevenson*)

Marriage is that relation between man and woman in which the independence is equal, the dependence mutual and the obligation reciprocal. (*L. K. Anspacher*)

Marriage is a lottery in which men stake their liberty and women their happiness. (*Mme. De Rieux*)

The secret of connubial bliss
Is not a felicitous kiss,
But this:
It is feckless and reckless
To discuss before breakfast. (*M. J. H.*)

Matrimony—the high sea for which no compass has yet been invented. (*H. Heine*)

May those who enter the rosy paths of matrimony never meet with thorns. (*Clotho*)

Marriage is the only venture open to the cowardly. (*Voltaire*)

LOVE

Love (charity) suffereth long and is kind; love envieth not; love vaunteth not itself, is not puffed up, Doth not behave itself unseemly, seeketh not her own, is not easily provoked, thinketh no evil; Rejoiceth not in iniquity, but rejoiceth in the truth; Beareth all things, believeth all things, hopeth all things, endureth all things. (*I Corinthians, 13, 4-7*)

First love is only a little foolishness and a lot of curiosity. (*G. B. Shaw*)

Love is biology set to music. (*M. J. H.*)

Love is an ocean of emotions entirely surrounded by expenses. (*Lord Dewar*)

Love consists in this, that two solitudes protect and touch and greet each other. (*Rilke*)

Love that giveth in full store
Aye receives as much, and more. (*D. M. M. Craik*)

All other things, to their destruction draw.
Only our love hath no decay. (*Donne*)

To be in love is merely to be in a state of perceptual anaesthesia —to mistake an ordinary young man for a Greek god or an ordinary young woman for a goddess. (*Mencken*)

Oh, 'tis love, 'tis love, that makes the world go round. (Carroll in *Alice's Adventures in Wonderland*)

WOMEN

Who can find a virtuous woman? for her price is far above rubies. (*Proverbs XXXI, 10*)

Her ways are ways of pleasantness and all her paths are peace. (*Proverbs III, 17*)

In her tongue is the law of kindness. (*Proverbs XXXI, 26*)

It is better to dwell in a corner of the housetop, than with a brawling woman in a wide house. (*Proverbs, XXI, 9*)

A continual dropping on a very rainy day and a contentious woman are alike. (*Proverbs XXVII, 15*)

Woman would be more charming if one could fall into her arms without falling into her hands. (*Bierce*)

Women are made to be loved; not to be understood. (*Oscar Wilde*)

The whole world is strewn with snares, traps, gins, and pitfalls for the capture of men by women. (*G. B. Shaw*)

Women would rather be right than reasonable. (*Ogden Nash*)

A woman is only a woman, but a good cigar is a smoke. (*Kipling*)

She's beautiful and therefore to be wooed,
She is a woman, therefore to be won. (*Shakespeare*)

A woman is necessarily an evil but he that gets the most tolerable is lucky. (*Menander, 343-292. B.C.*)

Ye must know that women have dominion over you: do ye not labour and toil, and give and bring all to the woman? (*The Apocrypha, I Esdras. IV, 22*)

Kindness in women, not their beauteous looks,
Shall win my love. (*Shakespeare*)

O, my luve is like a red red rose,
That's newly sprung in June.
O, my luve is like the melodie,
That's sweetly play'd in tune. (*Burns*)

Learning is nothing without cultivated manners, but when the two are combined in a woman you have one of the most exquisite products of civilization. (*Andre Maurois*)

Housekeeping in common is for women the acid test. (*Andre Maurois*)

There is no spectacle on earth more appealing than that of a beautiful woman in the act of cooking dinner for someone she loves. (*Thomas Wolfe*)

A Woman is a foreign land,
Of which, though there he settle young,
A man will ne'er quite understand
The customs, politics, and tongue. (*Coventry Patmore*)

There swims no goose so gray, but soon or late
She finds some honest gander for her mate. (*Pope*)

Woman, the only loved autocrat who elects without voting,
Governs without law, and decides without appeal. (*Clotho*)

Woman, the cause of most tempests that agitate mankind. (*J. J. Rousseau*)

A perfect woman, nobly planned,
To warm, to comfort and command. (*Wordsworth*)

Here's to the woman who has a smile for every joy, a tear for every sorrow, a consolation for every grief, an excuse for every fault, a prayer for every misfortune, and encouragement for every hope. (*Sainte-Foix*)

WIVES

Whoso findeth a wife findeth a good thing. (*Proverbs XVIII, 22*)

She looketh well to the ways of her household, and eateth not the bread of idleness. (*Proverbs, XXXI, 27*)

A wife is a big help. She helps her husband get out of the trouble he wouldn't have got into in the first place if he hadn't married. (*M. J. H.*)

Always talk to your husband as sweetly as you do to your butcher. (*M. J. H.*)

Every man who is high up loves to think that he has done it all himself; and his wife smiles and lets it go at that. (*J. M. Barrie*)

Behind every successful man stands a woman—nagging, nagging, nagging.

Behind every successful man stands a woman—surprised as hell. (*M. J. H.*)

Behind every unsuccessful man stands a woman—saying I told you so—and mother agrees. (*M. J. H.*)

Her children rise up and call her blessed. (*Proverbs, XXXI, 28*)

She's a winsome wee thing,
She's a handsome wee thing,
She is a lo'esome wee thing,
This sweet wee wife o' mine. (*Burns*)

To make a happy fireside clime
To weans and wife,
That's the true pathos and sublime
Of human life. (*Burns*)

HUSBANDS

Therefore shall a man leave his father and mother and shall cleave unto his wife, and they shall be one flesh. (*Genesis I, 24*)

Let the husband render unto the wife due benevolence: and likewise also the wife unto the husband. (*I Corinthians 7, 3*)

Advice to husbands—don't try to find out who is boss in the house—you'll be happier not knowing.

He tells you when you've got on too much lipstick,
And helps you with your girdle when your hips stick. (*Ogden Nash*)

There is only one thing for a man to do who is married to a woman who enjoys spending money, and that is to enjoy earning it. (*Edgar W. Howe*)

A successful man is one who can make more money than his wife can spend. A successful woman is one who can find such a man.

Bachelor—a man who shirks responsibilities and duties. (*G. B. Shaw*)

Romance—the only sport in which the animal that gets caught has to buy the license.

In days of old
   The knights I'm told
With their battle-axes parried.

But not all knights
   Got in such fights
Just the one's who were married. (*M. J. H.*)

Men sometimes say that women suffer from vanity. But until a woman can go around with a big bald spot on the back of her head and still think she's beautiful, she can't compare with a man for vanity.

Here's to the happy man: All the world loves a lover. (*Emerson*)

MISCELLANEOUS

If you start billing and cooing you're somebody's pigeon. (*M. J. H.*)

Mid pleasures and palaces though we may roam,
Be it ever so humble, there's no place like home. (*John Howard Payne*)

There is no place more delightful than home. (*Cicero, 100* B.C.)

This is the true nature of home—it is the place of peace; the shelter, not only from all injury, but from all terror, doubt and division. (*John Ruskin*)

Where we love is home,
Home that our feet may leave, but not our hearts. (*Oliver Wendell Holmes*)

What wisdom can you find that is greater than kindness. (*Rousseau*)

As is the mother, so is the daughter. (*Ezekiel XVI, 44*)

If everyone waited to have children until they could afford it the race would die out. (*M. J. H.*)

The wedding ring is worn by the wife but it cuts off the husband's circulation.

In marriage a woman gets a ring on her finger and the man gets a ring in his nose.

A diamond is made of carbon, the same as coal, but it burns with a hotter flame and an earlier ash. (*M. J. H.*)

Life isn't all beer and skittles. (*Thomas Hughes*)

Into each life some rain must fall. (*Longfellow*)

The weaker sex is the stronger sex because of the weakness of the stronger sex for the weaker sex.

The true male never yet walked
Who liked to listen when his mate talked. (*Anna Wickham*)

The battle of the sexes will never be fought to a conclusion—there is too much fraternization with the enemy.

Woman's intuition is the means by which she arrives at the wrong conclusion without the use of the fallacious reasoning she would otherwise use to arrive at the wrong conclusion. (*M. J. H.*)

Little puffs of powder, little dabs of paint,
Make the pretty girlies, look like what they ain't.

The slings and arrows of outrageous fortune. (*Shakespeare*)

No man is an island, entire of itself. (*Donne*)

All religion, all life, all art, all expression comes down to this: to the effort of the human soul to break through its barrier of loneliness, of intolerable loneliness, and make contact with another seeking soul, or with what all souls seek, which is (by any name) God. (*Marquis*)

Whatsoever things are true, whatsoever things are honest, whatsoever things are just, whatsoever things are pure, whatsocver things are lovely, whatsoever things are of good report; if there be any virtue, and if there be any praise, think on these. (*Philippians IV, 8*)

You are such a wonderful Baedeker to life. All the stars are in the right places. (*Elizabeth Asquith Bibesco*)

One can know nothing of giving ought that is worthy to give unless one also knows how to take. (*Havelock Ellis*)

Friends must understand
  Exchange of gifts is an art,
Give with an open hand,
  Receive with an open heart. (*M. J. H.*)

Same old slippers,
  Same old rice,
Same old glimpse of
  Paradise. (*W. J. Lampton*)

Gratitude is the sign of noble souls. (*Aesop*)

IV
Examples
of Toasts

EXAMPLE 1.

This toast is suitable for you regardless of your age in relation to that of the bride and groom, although preferably you should be somewhat older, and you need not know them well. This is an example of how to weave quotations into your remarks and how to use contrasting comments to advantage. Don't let cynicism win the day, however. You are on Cupid's side, remember, and you mustn't leave him looking foolish.

It has been said that being married is like sitting in the bathtub—after awhile it's not so hot. This is not true. It is my observation that when you are married you are in hot water all the time.

Marriage has been described in many ways by poets, sages, and scribes. Most of these, alas, seem to be critical and satirical, but then, after a picnic you remember the mosquitoes and not the butterflies. It is easier for a wit to be barbed than to be laudatory. It is remembered that Cervantes said, "Marriage is a noose," but who is remembered for having said marriage is a delight?

Ambrose Bierce has said, "Woman would be more charming if one could fall into her arms without falling into her hands." A cynic would say marriage makes a stoic. It has been said about women that men can't get along with them and can't get along without them. And love is described in a song as a tender trap. G. K. Chesterton is quoted as saying, "A marriage is neither an ecstasy nor a slavery; it is a commonwealth." That makes it sound awfully prosaic, doesn't it? Even the gentle R. L. Stevenson said, "Marriage is like life in this—that it is a field of battle, and not a bed of roses." I think R. L. S. should have stuck with his little shadow that went in and out with him. I'm inclined to think also that Voltaire might get a few arguments with his statement that, "Marriage is the only venture open to the cowardly."

There seems to be a tendency to regard marriage as all very well for women but a disaster for men. Disraeli said, "I respect the institution of marriage. I have always thought that every woman should marry and no man." It would appear that Disraeli wasn't very good at arithmetic. Shaw described the world as strewn with snares, traps, gins, and pitfalls for the capture of men by women. It has also been said that a man chases a girl until she catches him, and romance has been described as the only sport in which the animal that gets caught has to buy the license.

Are there then no favorable comments about marriage? Yes there are! Tennyson said, "Marriages are made in heaven." Ogden Nash has written, "Marriage is the only known example of the happy meeting of the immovable object and the irresistible force." I must confess I'm not sure whether that's favorable or not. There is nothing ambiguous about Thomas Wolfe when he says, "There is no spectacle on earth more appealing than that of a beautiful woman in the act of cooking dinner for someone she loves." And then we must come to Burns for the gentlest tribute to a wife:

> She is a winsome wee thing,
> She is a handsome wee thing,
> She is a lo'esome wee thing,
> This sweet wee wife o' mine.

So to the happy couple I would say, let your married life together be such as to confound the wits who would make fun of marriage and add support to those poets who sing its praises.

Let us rise now and drink confusion to the wits and joy to the happy couple. The happy couple.

EXAMPLE 2.

This example would be appropriate for a clergyman or an older friend of the family. He knows the bride and her family very well. The general tone is serious and the quotations are principally biblical. If you are quite young don't use this one, or you will appear like Elijah riding a bicycle.

It has been my privilege to see the bride we honor today grow from a tiny bundle of gurgles to the beautiful and radiant woman we see before us.

As a little girl Alice had qualities of gentleness, sweetness, generosity, and warmth that endeared her to all her friends. These qualities grew and deepened as she matured and she brings now this rich endowment to her fortunate husband in the marriage vows. If I would choose one word to describe the charm of her personality it would be kindness. She brings to her love, kindness. And it is my feeling that a beautiful and a kind woman is the good Lord's noblest creation.

Love can be lacking in kindness—it can be arrogant and demanding. But true love suffereth long and is kind; love envieth not; love vaunteth not itself, is not puffed up; Doth not behave itself unseemly, seeketh not her own, is not easily provoked, thinketh no evil; Rejoiceth not in iniquity, but rejoiceth in the truth; Beareth all things, believeth all things, hopeth all things, endureth all things. This is the love that Alice will bring to the formulation of her future home and household.

Love without kindness is selfish, and kindness without love is pretentious. Like the little girl said when describing love, "Love is giving the other person the biggest piece of cake." This is a good definition of the unselfishness that is a characteristic of love. Love is the noblest of virtues, and kindness is the sweetest manifestation of love. In the Book of Proverbs it says, "Who can find a virtuous woman? for her price is far above rubies." And elsewhere it records, "In her tongue is the law of kindness" and "Her ways are ways of pleasantness and all her paths are peace." In balance it must be admitted that the Book of Proverbs also describes a household where kindness does not prevail, in these words: "It is better to dwell in a corner of a housetop, than with a brawling woman in a wide house." But we shall have none of that and Alec, we know, will not have to take to the housetop.

Later poets through the years have paid tribute to the virtue of kindness in women. Shakespeare expressed it this way, "Kindness in women, not their beauteous looks, shall win my love." How fortunate is our bridegroom to have found both beauty and kindness in the same person. And fortunate is Alice in finding a young man worthy of her gifts, for he brings treasure of character in equal abundance.

One writer has soundly equated wisdom and kindness when he wrote, "What wisdom can you find that is greater than kindness?" And I say, happy and blessed is the home where love abides and kindness holds domain. Our happy couple will have such a home, and fortunate indeed are they.

And now in raising our glasses in their honor let me maintain the theme of kindness and quote the greatest love poet of them all, Robert Burns: "We'll take a cup o' kindness yet for auld lang syne!" To the bride.

EXAMPLE 3.

This example might be used by an older person and he need not know the bride or groom well as there are few personal references. The general tone is serious. This toast demonstrates how you may follow a theme throughout—in this case, "We would wish for you . . ." This theme could also be used in a lighter vein.

We are assembled here today to express to the happy couple our best wishes for their future. There are many, many things we would wish for you, Mary and George. Let me try to list some of these.

We would wish for you happiness. But what do we mean by happiness? True and deep happiness has many parts. It is composed of joy and grief, gaiety and sorrow, gladness and woe. We would not wish that you experience no sadness, no cares. It would be impractical—and unfair. For the moments of sadness add poignancy to the joys; failures add sweetness to triumphs; and difficulties add zest to accomplishments. The shadows emphasize the sunlight. So may your problems be manageable, may you have contentment without complacency, and may you have a good balance of joy over sadness. Then will your happiness be rich, and deep and abiding.

Next we would wish for you courage and strength. When couples marry they give hostages to fortune and increase their vulnerability to the slings and arrows of outrageous fortune. We would wish for you then the courage and strength to meet the challenges of life and to withstand the knocks and buffeting that Fate may give you.

We would wish for you good health, so that you may live long and live fully, free of the pain and distress of sickness, and the woes that the flesh is subject to.

We would wish for you prosperity. But may it not come so fast that you do not savor the getting of it, nor in such abundance that you forget the joys of simplicity and frugality. A groom said to his bride, "Someday we shall be wealthy." She answered, "We are wealthy; someday we shall have money."

We would wish for you a family so that you may complete the circle at your fireside and pass on the richness of your love and heritage to the future.

We would wish for you a warm circle of friends, for friends are the most valuable treasures you will collect throughout your life. Turn your love outward and you will find other human beings to share and enrich your life. Keep your friendships in repair and do not take them for granted. Cherish your old friendships, but seek always new ones.

We would wish for you tolerance and intolerance, tolerance for the foibles of each other and for the weaknesses of your friends, but intolerance for bigotry, pettiness, arrogance, and all things mean and contemptible.

We would wish for you wisdom, the wisdom to seek always for whatsoever things are true, whatsoever things are honest, whatsoever things are just, whatsoever things are pure, whatsoever things are lovely. You must have the wisdom to value what is worthy and to despise what is unworthy.

We would wish for you an ever growing appreciation of the love and mercy of God.

These and many more things we would wish for our young friends in their life ahead. Would you rise now and pledge these good wishes in a toast to the happy couple.

EXAMPLE 4.

This example would be used by an older person since it employs rather serious advice and comment. He knows the couple fairly well. The story about the piglets has a special significance to me since it actually was told by the minister at my parents' wedding.

Many, many years ago when my mother and father were married the minister described marriage in the following way. (I hasten to mention that I was not there—I was told about it.) Anyhow, the minister compared marriage with a farmer feeding hot mash to his piglets. Each little pig ran up to the trough and stuck his nose in it and got burned and ran squealing away. But every other piglet ran up and got his nose burned too.

Now is it possible to be married and not go around with a band-aid on your nose? Yes, it is. In successful marriages no one gets his nose burned. But successful marriages don't happen by accident and they won't function automatically. Marriage is the most important relationship in a person's life and as such it is worthy of the best attention, thought, and efforts of those involved. Ibsen has said, "Marriage is a thing you've got to give your whole mind to." Marriage is not a hobby to be taken up in spare moments. Marriage is a full-time, life-time proposition that needs to be studied and worked at to make it a success. With love, goodwill, and good sense success is assured. Then all other accomplishments are enhanced and disappointments are minimized.

Life is not all beer and skittles and of course the sea of matrimony blows up quite a storm occasionally. Sure, there will be spats and squabbles. That's part of the fun—particularly the making-up part. In the words of A. P. Herbert, "The conception of two people living together for 25 years without having a cross word suggests a lack of spirit only to be admired in sheep." So don't be alarmed if sparks fly once in awhile; just don't let them start a fire and burn down the house. It takes two to tango and two to tangle.

Some simple words of kindly advice for the bride:
> Now listen please my darling daughter
> Keeping your husband in hot water
> As far as anyone can ever remember
> Never did much to render him tender.

And now to be fair, some advice to the groom:

Although it has been said:
> The true male never yet walked
> Who liked to listen when his mate talked.
> Yet it is a good idea once in awhile to sit
> her down and give her a real good listening to.

And to both of you, remember:
> The sweetest words of pen or song
> Are these
> You are right and I was wrong.

If you follow my advice I'm sure you will become good friends. This may sound like a strange thing to say, but I mean it. Just because you're married doesn't mean you can't be friends. There is such a thing as liking each other as well as loving each other. You're going to spend a lot of time together in the next umpteen years so it will be a big help if you enjoy each other's company. So try to make yourself worthy of being a friend. A person who is a likable friend is charming, affable, and fun to be with. Do not lean on love; it is not a crutch for an emotional weakling.

This is a happy day for all of us, and undoubtedly the happiest day in the lives of Ruth and Dick. This is an auspicious beginning of what we know will be many days and many years of happiness. What fun you will have in facing life together establishing a new home, meeting challenges, forming new friendships! And the happiness that each of you will feel will be doubled, nay tripled, nay multiplied many times, by the sharing of it.

Also we must concede that into each life some rain must fall. Things would be dry as dust otherwise. But sorrows are minimized by communion, just as joys are richer by being shared. Until you have mingled your tears together you are not really married—you are just batching together. Shared sorrows like shared joys are part of married life. And shared tears form the cement which holds a husband and wife together.

Let us rise now and raise our glasses in a toast to the happy bride and groom. May long life and happiness be theirs.

EXAMPLE 5.

The proposer of this toast is an older person who knows the families of both the bride and groom well and makes use of the knowledge. It demonstrates how you may take a theme and develop it; in this case, the idea of establishing a new home. Also it shows how you may work in charming marriage customs from other societies.

In the marriage today of Patricia and Allan we see the union of two fine families it has been my privilege to know for many years. Our bride and bridegroom are fortunate indeed to come from homes with such a fine tradition of warmth, kindliness, love, and godliness. But now they must forsake all others and cleave only unto each other. They do, however, carry with them the training and tradition of their family homes in the establishment of their own home.

What is a home? A house may be built in a day but it takes a heap of living and a heap of loving to create a home. It is not the roof, the walls, and the shining chrome that go to make a home. The roof may leak, the walls may be askew, and the plumbing erratic, but it is a home if there is love within. Cicero away back in 100 B.C. said, "There is no place more delightful than home." Someone has said, home is where you hang your hat, but that is wrong; home is where the heart is. Home is the loveliest word in the English language. Now why is that so? Because it epitomizes all that we hold dearest to our hearts and is the embodiment of unselfish love. Ruskin has said, "This is the true nature of home: it is the place of peace; the shelter, not only from all injury, but from all terror, doubt, and division." Building such a sanctuary is a challenging project requiring patience, understanding, tolerance, and good humor. A charming part of the nuptial rites of the Narrinyeri in Australia is a custom where the woman signifies her consent to the marriage by carrying fire to her husband's hut, and making his fire for him. Patricia in a way does this symbolically today in that she brings to her new home a spark of the warmth from her old home to kindle a new hearth to warm the heart by.

This is a proud day for us all. The families are proud; we are proud; and Patricia and Allan are proud. Not proud in the sense of arrogant pride that cometh before a fall, but a pride humble and grateful. We delight and rejoice in the happiness of the bride and bridegroom. Allan, you may be humbly proud of the love that Patricia has bestowed upon you and the trust she has placed in you. And Patricia, you may be grateful for the love of a fine and worthy young man.

Ladies and gentlemen, will you raise your glasses in a salutation to the happy couple and the establishment of a new and happy home.

EXAMPLE 6.

This toast is based on a musical motif and shows how you may make use of a particular interest of the bride and groom. You need to be sure that most of the audience will understand the vocabulary or they may not tune in on your wavelength (A 440). However, if the bride and groom have a particularly strong interest, it is probable that many of their friends will share it. You need not devote the entire talk to one theme as I have done here. You can use a similar approach with other areas of interest such as painting, dancing, photography, etc.

Our bride and groom both have the great good fortune to be well versed in the realms of music. If, as it is said, music is the food of love, then their married relationship will be well nourished. Let us follow up this musical motif.

We would hope they would always be in harmony, with no significant dissonances. However, we recognize that the occasional discord adds sweetness to the following concord so let the euphony be sharpened a little from time to time with subtle discords. But no *fortissimo sostenuto* cacophonies. They need not always play in unison but let the counterpoint be judicious and blend into a melodious obbligato. May they always play in the same key and may their troubles be minor and their joys major. We would hope for a natural harmony with no sharp words and no flat moments.

Their rhythms should synchronize and coordinate and neither member of the duo should come down heavy on the upbeat. Some syncopation is to be expected but one of them must not launch off on a martial 6/8 while the other is Straussing up a 3/4.

Let them take turns singing the solo part and let each occasionally lend the other accompaniment. The tones should be always mellifluous with no overtones of malice and of a proper balance so that one does not drown out the other. Let the soprano never become shrill or strident nor the bass become a grumble or a growl. We realize that at the beginning of this lifelong concert they will be singing duets only, but we hope that in due time they will have a whole substantial choir to swell the chorus.

The musical directions to be followed in their songs to each other are *dolce, contabile, vivace, amabile,* and *con tenerezza* with a little *appassionata* and *amoroso.*

The directions to be avoided are, *furioso,* and *lamentoso.* And we hope in their music together there will be no *doloroso* or *mesto.*

Sometimes in any family duet there are harsh notes that one is tempted to sound, but refrain and play these *tacet*—or as the fiddle players say, with soap on the bow.

May the chords that join them always be as well tempered as a clavichord and may pleasures be dominant, troubles diminished, and joys augmented.

Now let us drink to our two happy *virtuosos.* May their song of love be a rhapsody and may they make beautiful music together.

EXAMPLE 7.

In this toast the speaker need not know the couple well since personal references are avoided. If you use the "loneliness" theme, counterbalance it with a zestful section or you may appear to imply that the only reason for getting married is not to be lonely.

Let us first take a philosophic look at marriage. Philosophers disagree on many things but on one point they are mostly agreed —that loneliness is the saddest affliction that can pervade the human soul. Marriage has many virtues, but one of the chief of these is that it insures against loneliness. You may be a lot of other things, but you won't be lonely.

The poet expresses the same idea in a different way when he says that no man is an island, entire of itself; and the theologian says, it is not good that man should be alone. It is natural then for each human soul to endeavor to break through its barrier of loneliness and make contact with another seeking soul. Marriage offers an opportunity for such a contact and it is held together by the powerful forces of love and trust and shared dreams. Some sense of isolation must always remain and there is in each person a corner of his soul that is forever private. The wise person does not intrude. Rilke has said, "Love consists in this, that two solitudes protect and touch and greet each other." And Gibran says, "Let there be spaces in your togetherness." Thus, loneliness is not eliminated by marriage, but is made tolerable.

But marriage has many *positive* attributes as well. It is an excitement, a challenge, and a joy. We have here two happy people full of the zest for life. Oh, what a fine life they will have together! They have the exuberance and the courage to meet any difficulties; the warmth, charm, and good humor to make and hold fine friendships; the tolerance and good sense to get along well together; and most important of all, the warmth of their deep love to form a happy home.

We are happy for them. We delight in their happiness. We wish them long life and prosperity.

Will you all rise now and drink a toast to the happy couple.

EXAMPLE 8.

This toast would be appropriate for an older person who need not know the couple well. It uses a consistent theme throughout—the wine of love.

We have today been witnesses at a marriage. Marriage has its basis in love. What then is this thing called love (to quote a song) that produces this remarkable denouement?

Love has been described in many ways. It is an itch you can't scratch; it is what makes the world go round; it is biology set to music; it is an intoxicating wine. If it is the latter, then marriage is the chalice that holds the wine of love.

This chalice is a magic cup. It continually renews the essences which it contains so that it is always full to the brim. It preserves the wine of love so that it is always clean and fresh. It imparts to the draught healing qualities so that it soothes the heart-sick, heals the hurt, and refreshes the weary. And most important of all, the marriage chalice improves the wine with age. A couple will find that as the years go by and they cherish their marriage, the wine of their love will be mellowed and enriched; it will be sweeter, more full bodied, and of a more poignant bouquet.

Wine of love without the marriage goblet is a sporting potion only—a trivial and transitory intoxicant. It is soon depleted, soon diluted with tears, soon flat, stale, and turned to vinegar.

Fortunate then are the couple who treasure their marriage cup. The happy couple we see before us have today been given such a cup, blessed by God and received in the presence of their friends. It is fitting then that we raise our own emblematic glasses in their honor.

I ask you now to rise and drink a toast to the happy couple.

EXAMPLE 9.

This toast is facetious and could be used by a young friend of the couple who knows them well. Considerable skill as a raconteur would be required to put it across, so unless you have had some speaking experience you had better not try this one or you will end up like a skunk in a hen-house with egg on your face. You could tell the story not using quotes and it would be easier, although less effective.

Marriage is a product of civilization and necessary to its maintenance. Man is not naturally monogamous. He is not even naturally polygamous. He is sort of whoopyogamous. Woman is monogamous because she needs one person to take the responsibility of protecting the nest. The nest is essential to the maintenance of civilization. Into woman's hands then has been placed the future of society. She must tame and halter these male brutes. The device she uses is marriage.

Let us look back into our primordial past and see how the whole thing started. Great-great-to-the-nth-power grandfather was sitting on a branch up in a tree, eating a banana and waving languidly at the girl apes in the next tree. Great-great-to-the-nth-power grandmother was sitting on another branch thinking —always a dangerous thing in a woman. She finally turned to great-great-to-the-nth-power grandfather and said, "George, let's climb down out of this tree and start the human race."

Great-great-to-nth-power grandfather said, "Ah shuks, Mable, I'm happy just sitting on this here little old branch."

"I know you are George. That's what's wrong with you, no gumption," said great-great-to-the-nth-power grandmother. "If we don't get things started there won't be any human race."

"No good will come of it believe me," said George. "And furthermore if we climb down out of this tree we will get chased by lions and tigers and lawyers and bill collectors and other vicious animals."

"George!" said great-great-to-the-nth-power grandmother.

"Oh, all right, Mable, if it will make you happy," said great-great-to-the-nth-power grandfather. "So long girls," he said to the girl apes in the next tree.

"So long, George," they answered. And how right they were.

So great-great-to-the-nth-power grandfather grumbled and grumbled but he climbed down out of that tree.

"And now, George," said great-great-to-the-nth-power grandmother, "the first thing we have to do is get married."

"Married?" said great-great-to-the-nth-power grandfather. "What's that?"

"You'll find out," said great-great-to-the-nth-power grandmother. And she smiled enigmatically to herself.

So that's how it all started.

And so today we see this ancient tradition being carried on. I ask you now to rise and drink a toast to grandmother's great-great-to-the-nth-power granddaughter—the bride.

EXAMPLE 10.

This toast is presented in a light-hearted vein and could be given by a contemporary or an older person. The subject of marriage is considered from several points of view, some of which will require special knowledge in your audience. The designation of a wife as the "leader of the loyal opposition" in the family house of parliament would be lost in a country where this British terminology is not used.

How may we describe a marriage? In the world of business we would say it is a partnership. A board of directors with two chairmen, two controllers, and two shareholders—all the same people. All decisions must therefore be unanimous. A young couple after their marriage discussed how decisions should be arrived at. It was agreed that she would make the minor decisions and he the major decisions. Several years later a friend asked the husband how this had worked out. He replied, "Just fine. So far there have been no major decisions."

Now Edward is a businessman and he is familiar with the term "*caveat emptor*" (let the buyer beware), and maybe it is applicable here because he has certainly sold Kathleen a bill of goods. But this is one time when a businessman really stands behind his goods and he is his own guarantee. We know he will deliver.

Next, let us consider philosophy. Philosophy is the search for truth. And this Kathleen and Edward have found when they looked into each others eyes. Foolish philosophers search in the sky or in the desert, not knowing that the greatest truth is found in lovers' eyes.

But let us leave these philosophical concepts and turn to the world of sport. Kathleen and Edward are now a team and teamwork is essential. Does a quarterback trip his own half back? Does a pitcher stick his finger in the catcher's eye? Does a defence man steal the puck from his own forward? Does a forward try to score on his own goalie? No indeed. And a wise captain or co-captain will wait until the privacy of the club house is reached before reaming out a teammate for errors or shortcomings. People are seldom persuaded of error by being shouted at, and coaching is best handled in gentle tones. Adjustments are rarely arrived at in public and agreements never reached in a loud voice.

And now to turn to science. Marriage is not a mutual phagocytosis wherein each engulfs the other. The cellular morphology remains distinct, but a new organism is formed in the conjoining. In chemical terms we might say, this atom Edward and this atom Kathleen have found an affinity and have decided to share electrons to form a new molecule. In jet-age terminology we could describe marriage as a rendezvous in space of two happy souls. Or in piscatorial parlance we would say marriage is fish and fisherman caught in the same net. Who is which, I shall leave an open question.

In British policital terms we could say that we have today convened a new house of parliament with Edward the prime minister and Kathleen the leader of the loyal opposition.

So you see the union we have witnessed today is fortunate indeed. It has a sound basis in business, philosophy, sport, science and politics.

Let us rise and drink to their success in all these fields. The happy couple.

EXAMPLE 11.

This toast is presented as a fairy tale and could only be given by an old friend of the family who knew the bride well all her life. It would require considerable skill in story telling to be effective.

Today I am going to tell you a fairy tale. Once upon a time there was an enchanted castle. Now this castle wasn't in a deep forest. In fact it was right in a big city. And to look at it, maybe you wouldn't know right away that it was an enchanted castle because it looked quite a bit like an ordinary bungalow. But it was enchanted by the magic of the love and kindness of the people who lived in it.

Then one day into this happy family was born a little princess and she was called Betty and there was great rejoicing. And Betty grew up in this castle and was given all the training appropriate for a princess: schooling, dancing, music, sports, and also an appreciation of her responsibilities to God and to her fellow beings. And Betty added a magic of her own to the household with the sunshine of her laughter, the sparkle of her eyes, and the charm of her personality.

In this castle there also lived two mischievous elves who were her brothers and they played a lot of tricks on Betty. One time they took away the ladder after Betty and a friend had climbed to the top of the garage and left them there for a long time. The elves had their bottoms paddled for this but they went right on being mischievous.

In any fairy story there must be a wicked old ogre—and there was one. He lived in a house down the street and he was very proud of his flower garden. One day the little princess sneaked into the garden and she cut the heads off a lot of his daffodils. And the old ogre came rampaging out of the house breathing fire and smoke and roaring like a dragon. The princess ran away home, but she came back later and said she was very sorry and she and the old ogre have been very good friends ever since. Haven't we Betty?

In due time the little princess grew up into beautiful womanhood and she was renowned throughout the land, for she was not only beautiful but also kind and sweet and charming. And so great was her renown that many handsome princes and suitors came to the castle to offer their hearts to her. There were many parties and dancing and merriment but she did not give her hand to any of these. Then one day along came a handsome knight in shining armor riding a great white horse. Now I must admit that the armor was an old Phi Delt T-shirt and the white horse was really a beat-up, old Chevrolet but this is a fairy tale and the magic is still upon us. This prince charming swept our little princess off her feet and they decided to start an enchanted castle of their own.

So our little princess appears today before us as the happy bride and we all wish for her what fairy tales always end with: "And they lived happily ever after."

Ladies and gentlemen: nobles, dukes, duchesses, all, please rise and drink a toast to our favorite princess, Betty, the bride.

EXAMPLE 12.

This toast would be given by an older friend since it undertakes to give some blunt advice, although in a light manner. This is for you if you are a bluff, no-nonsense type of person.

I am not going to indulge in any deep philosophical considerations of the married state, but rather give some blunt, down-to-earth advice on how to get along together; in other words, how to be happy though married.

First, a poem.

> The secret of connubial bliss
> Is not a felicitous kiss,
> But this,
> It is feckless and reckless
> To discuss before breakfast.

And always squeeze the toothpaste from the bottom.

So much for the morning and now for night. Never go to bed mad. If you have had a row don't close the day hugging your rancor. You both will be sore of heart, so let your love heal the hurt and tomorrow is another day.

Take turns being cranky. We can't all be sweet all of the time, so if one is being ornery let the other be gentle. If he is in a foul temper, stand well back; and if she is in a bad mood, take to the hills. These moods blow themselves out if allowed to do so.

Plan for the future but don't live in the future. Have fun as you go along. Vulgar finances always raise their head in any family. Don't be alarmed, talk it out. There's nothing like a good big mortgage to hold a family together. Do your budgeting carefully, but always allow something for frivolity. Take her out for dinner once in a while; buy a bouquet of roses for no good reason; buy him a new pipe he doesn't need. When children come along let them be delights and not tyrants—you still have a duty to each other.

If a horse is given a loose rein he will always head for home. So Peggy, let Jake go out with the boys once in a while. It is the nature of the beasts that men must join together occasionally for man talk and poker, or golf, or such. He'll come back happily.

And Jake, let Peggy go out with the girls. After a few hours in a magpie nest she will delight in your company.

Don't try to score on one another. One-up-manship has no place in marriage. Don't fuss about things that don't really matter and don't make a point just to make a point. Don't try to find out who is boss; you will both be happier not knowing. If one of you is wrong it isn't always essential that this be pointed out. If you can't say something nice, keep quiet. A wife should always speak as sweetly to her husband as she does to her butcher.

Don't be chary with compliments. If you are proud of something he did, say so. If you like her new hat, say so. If you don't like her new hat, say you do anyhow. A certain amount of dishonesty is essential to any good marriage.

Keep in communication. Don't nag, natter or whine; but don't encase yourself in an icy deepfreeze. You don't have to talk all the time, but maintain a rapport. One of the delights of married life is companionable silence.

Never correct each other in public. If he says, "A year ago on our holidays we bumped into the Fregbees in New York," don't say, "It was two years ago and it was in Honolulu," even if you're right, or particularly if you're right. It doesn't really matter and you've made him look like a chump. Never contradict, never butt in, and don't steal each other's punch lines. Never belittle or poke fun at your beloved in front of others. If he doesn't return your opening lead in bridge when you are sitting with a missing suit, don't make him out an idiot even if he is one. And never, never, play your bridge game over after you get home.

Accept and, preferably, share each other's hobbies and enthusiasms. If he's nuts about camping and your idea of roughing it is the Imperial in Tokyo, try to develop an enthusiasm for creepy, crawly things in your sleeping bag. If she is wild about symphony music, and you don't know an oboe from a pool cue, at least go uncomplaining to the concerts. You can have a quiet snooze and who knows? You might even get to like Beethoven.

All this is fairly mundane advice. But what does it boil down to? To this: Let your love be kind, good humored, and tolerant. If it is you can't help but be happy.

Ladies and gentlemen, raise your glasses and drink a toast to the continued happiness of a wonderful couple.

EXAMPLE 13.

The speaker using this toast would be an older person (see reference to myopia of age) although a younger person could use much of the material. The toast requires that he know both bride and groom well.

The die is cast, the ship is launched, the I dos are done, the knot is tied. This is a happy beginning of a joyful life together for Margaret and Fred. Our bride and groom today have taken out an insurance policy against loneliness and unhappiness. Be sure to keep up the payments or the policy will lapse. And what are the payments? Love and good will. That's all. What marvelous dividends the policy pays in happiness, security, and delight! Furthermore, the dividends increase from year to year in geometric progression by interest compounded daily. Fort Knox should have it so good!

You can cast your bread upon the waters and get back nothing but soggy bread; you can shoot an arrow in the sky and lose your arrow; you can eat your cake and get a stomach ache; but when you give your heart you are using your head, for, as the poet says:

> Love that giveth in full store
> Aye receives as much and more.

So we congratulate Margaret and Fred for their great good sense in falling in love and in choosing each other, for if love is to be fulfilled the recipients must be worthy. This we have in our happy couple today. Now how did this happen?

From a strictly statistical point of view the correct choice in a marriage is an impossibility. If there is one right man for each right girl, then out of the millions on this earth there is no statistical probability that they will ever even meet. Furthermore, the choice of a marriage partner, the most vital decision of a person's life, is made under the stress of emotions that render rational thought impossible. But Margaret and Fred have confounded statistics, have confounded rationality, for they are just exactly right for each other. So we don't know how or why it happened, but we are just glad it did. If there are some lovers that are star-crossed, then it follows there are some lovers for whom all the stars are in their right places. And we don't have to be very perceptive to see the stars shining in their eyes.

How lucky we are today to be able to get a glimpse of life through the starry eyes of our bride and groom. No myopia of age, no astigmatism of disillusionment; just a clear view of things through the rose-colored glasses of love. A cynic has said that to be in love is to be in a state of perceptual anaesthesia; to mistake an ordinary young man for a Greek god or an ordinary young woman for a goddess. But he is wrong. It is only through the eyes of love that we see people as they really are. Furthermore, our bride and groom are not ordinary young people but star-blessed, as we have proven, and even we can see the nimbus of Olympus hovering around their heads.

I ask you to rise now and drink a toast to the starry-eyed stars of the day. The happy couple.

EXAMPLE 14.

This example demonstrates how to string song titles together to tell a story. You can use a song of particular significance to the couple ("their" song), or to the group, and may substitute titles currently popular and well known to your audience. You would probably be advised not to give the whole toast in this way, as I have done here, as the novelty may pall, but you may use the idea as part of your talk. You can do the same sort of thing with titles of books, plays, movies, or even advertising slogans.
Dear Hearts and Gentle People:

Since our bride comes from a musical family I shall tell you a bit about her by using song titles. *We'll Turn Around* and take a *Sentimental Journey* into *Yesterday's Memories* when *Happy Days Are Here Again* and *Sweet Sue** was just a *Cry Baby* and a *Cutie Pants*. We can say *You Must Have Been a Beautiful Baby 'cause Baby Look at You Now*. Our *Baby Doll* loved her *Home Sweet Home* and went on to *School Days* with reading, 'riting, and 'rithmetic. She was *Forever Blowing Bubbles* and playing *London Bridge is Falling Down* and *Hop Scotch*. Later she left her *Rocking Horse* for *Rock and Roll* and was a little *Goofus*.

Ah, but *Love is Just Around the Corner* with *That Old Black Magic* and then *Love Walked In*. It was *Oh, Johnny** all *Smiles*, saying *Be My Little Bumble Bee* and *Gimmie a Little Kiss, Will Ya, Huh?* He was *Whispering, Tenderly, Loves Old Sweet Song, I'm Confessing that I Love You, Forever and Ever* so *Please, Girl of My Dreams, Let Me Call You Sweetheart. Be My Life's Companion* and *We'll Go Marching along Together, Side by Side* to a *Little Gray Home in the West* or a *Little Grass Shack in Kealakekua, Hawaii*.

Sweet Sue was *Bewitched* and *All Shook Up*. She knew *A Good Man Is Hard to Find* and *It's So Nice to Have a Man Around the House* but *Never on Sunday*. She said *I've Got a Feeling I'm Falling* and *Now I Know What Is This Thing Called Love. I Love You Truly, Heart and Soul*, so I'll be your *Toot Toot Tootsie* for *Always*. So it was *Love and Marriage* and *Lohengrin*.

And now Sue and John, on the *Long, Long Trail Awinding* ahead *For You* to the time when there are *Silver Threads Among the Gold* we hope you *Always* have *Blue Skies* on the *Sunny Side of the Street* and no *Stormy Weather*. No *Heartaches*, no *Mistakes* and no *Blues in the Night*. And *Some of these Days, Remember* to look back at today and say *Thanks for the Memories*.

Ladies and Gentlemen. A toast to the happy couple.

---

*Songs with other names: Marie, Barbara, Margie, Donna, Clementine, Laura, Brenda, Josephine, Irene, Mary, Peggy, Louise, Anna, Gloria, Jim, Elmer, Mike, Andy, Mac (the Knife), Bill (Bailey), Randy, Ronnie, Tommy, etc.

EXAMPLE 15.

Toast by the best man or the chairman. Sometimes the toast to the bride is given by the best man. The best man has been selected as such because of his close association with the groom. If he also knows the bride well, his toast may be similar to those described elsewhere. If he does not, he simply expresses best wishes for success and happiness. If the toast is by the chairman, or if the best man is also chairman, he is not introduced but exercises the prerogative of his position to propose the toast. The toast may be very simple. Here are two examples:

Ladies and gentlemen. Please rise and drink a toast to the loveliest of brides.

Ladies and gentlemen. We are gathered here to honor this happy couple on this, the first day of what we hope for them is to be a long and happy life together. Let us now pay tribute to this lovely bride who has made our friend Bob the luckiest of men.

I ask you now to rise and drink with me a toast to the bride. To the bride.

EXAMPLE 16.

This example is appropriate for a person the same age as the bride and groom. You may use the device of quoting other people's remarks, real or imaginary. You needn't be hampered by veracity. If you are a classical scholar you may go on a tour of Hades and interview the shades of great lovers, Lothario, Don Juan, H. Q. Snodgrass, etc. Be sure however, your audience can make the trip with you and not get stuck in the Styx.

It is my delightful responsibility to propose the toast to our beautiful bride Patricia. I shall also include a few remarks about Paul, my good friend, the lucky groom.

When I recovered from the great pleasure I felt at being asked to perform this function, I realized that I didn't have an ink in the inkling or a clue in the clues closet what I should say. As I am about the same age as the bride and groom, I am not in a position to bring the prestige of seniority to the job and further-more, I am not even married so I can hardly offer advice. How-ever, not knowing what I am talking about has never bothered me particularly and I shall press on in fearless ignorance.

The first thing I did was look up marriage in the dictionary. I had a pretty good idea what it was all about, but I thought I should make sure. The only thing helpful I found there was that in cards, marriage is the declaration of the king and queen of the same suit. This certainly seems to fit today because we have before us the king and queen of hearts. The ace is low, there are no trumps, and there's nothing wild.

My next step was to consult with people who were older and, I hoped, wiser than I am. I first asked my Uncle Will what he thought about marriage. Now Uncle Will is a bachelor so maybe this wasn't the best choice in the world. Uncle Will said, "Mar-riage? Why buy a picture when you can wander through the art galleries free? Why buy a book when the libraries are open? Why buy a mannequin when you can window shop? Why. . . ." I interrupted with "All right," Already I could see this wasn't going to be too helpful.

So next I asked Uncle Henry, who is married, what to watch out for in a marriage. He said, "If she has the dish towels em-broidered His and His, don't marry her. Remember, when you carry her over the threshold, the first thing she does is put her foot down."

Next I decided to seek out a philosopher. You might think this means I went to the university. Far from it. I went to a bar down on State Street. You find more philosophers and more sensible philosophy in a bar than you ever will in the ivory tower. I met in the bar an old philosopher, and I told him my mission and asked what he thought of marriage. He said, "Any-one who gets married has a hole in his head. But anyone who doesn't get married has a hole in his heart." I said "Thank you, Socrates." And he said, "How did you know my name, boy?"

Then I took my problem to my mother as I have all my life.

She and Dad have been happily married for twenty-eight years and I asked her the secret of her happiness. She answered, "A girl should marry a man as wonderful as your father." Then I asked Dad the same question, and do you know what he said? He said, "Marry someone as wonderful as your mother."

At last I had found the secret! Marry someone who you think is wonderful and keep right on thinking it. I can tell by looking at Patricia that she thinks Paul is pretty wonderful, and I have some inside information that Paul thinks Patricia is just about the most wonderful thing that ever walked. So you two just hold onto that, and I know you will, and you will have a happy, happy married life.

Ladies and gentlemen, lift your glasses and drink a toast to two wonderful people, the bride and groom.

EXAMPLE 17.

Suitable for a contemporary of the bride and groom. The purpose here is to demonstrate how you may make use of some humorous incident that happened during the courting days of the couple. Or you may describe how they happened to meet, as in this example. Couples often meet originally under circumstances that are interesting to recall, and not infrequently by devious stratagems of friends—usually female.

I must be young and foolish to have accepted the formidable challenge of doing justice to proposing a toast to so lovely a bride. How can I adequately salute the beauty of such a bride and the gallantry of such a groom? But I am so fond of them both that I accepted with alacrity this opportunity to pay them tribute. So please be aware I am doing my best and my heart is doing graceful pirouettes even if my number twelves are clomping all over the petunia patch.

When I asked my Blue-eyed Gumdrop, that's my wee wifey, what I should say, she replied, "Honey, you could recite the phone book and be a sensation." I sure would be. Anyhow that's a good first lesson for a bride. Tell your husband he's wonderful even if he is a donkey.

My Blue-eyed Gumdrop and I would like to think we can take credit for the happy event of today. It happened this way. At one of the biweekly board meetings in our household it developed that my wife had a dear friend named Marie who she thought was wonderful and I mentioned I had a friend who was a pretty good type named Jock. So the Chairman of the Board got a far-away look in her pretty blue eyes and took the matter under advisement. The way nature abhors a vacuum has nothing on the way a married woman resents an eligible bachelor roaming around loose. This is for two reasons: it is an affront to her sex; and also her husband is apt to start wondering if he did the right thing and get restive. So a plot evolved. Now as a plotter I'm strictly a Guy Fawkes but as a conniver it developed my Blue-eyed Gumdrop makes Machiavelli look like Humpty Dumpty. Well, in due time Marie and Jock met in our living room one evening. At about ten o'clock my Blue-eyed Gumdrop fixed me with a knowing look and said, "Oh Honey, I forgot I have to run over to see mother. Will you drive me?" I said, "What for? You saw your mother this afternoon, I, yi, yi . . ." You'd be surprised how steely blue eyes can get sometimes. I got the message. The idea, which was conveyed to me in the car, was to leave Marie and Jock alone together so they would see how nice a little comfy home of their own would be.

We got back in about an hour and the feathers had hit the fan. Our one year old had wakened up and was shouting the roof down. The man from the diaper service had arrived with a bill which had been unpaid, for reasons that may occur to you, and Jock had given him a check. And something had boiled over on the stove and the place was full of smoke. What a shambles! Marie and Jock left rather promptly I thought.

So you can plainly see we were a big help in getting their romance off to a good start. In spite of our help they decided to get married anyhow.

One problem Jock won't have is like the man said after seeing all the pretty girls at Las Vegas, "I wonder if my wife belongs to the same species." Marie makes any chorus girl I ever saw look like Charles de Gaulle. It is said that beauty is in the eye of the beholder. All I can add is that it sure helps to have a good stimulus. As you can all so abundantly see today, Marie is beautiful. But she wears her beauty gracefully—not as a weapon nor a shield, nor a substitute for inner grace. Inside this beautiful package is a truly lovely person. The external charm and radiance is a reflection only of her inner warmth and kindness and gentleness. Jock is a fortunate man.

But what then of my good friend Jock? Is he worthy of such riches? Yes he is. I've known Jock for many years and I am proud that he counts me among his friends. They don't come any better than Jock MacNab and even my little Blue-eyed Gumdrop agrees. These are my two favorite people and I am delighted to see them join together.

So ladies and gentlemen, raise your glasses and drink a toast to the favorite people of all of us. May long life and happiness be theirs. The happy couple.

EXAMPLE 18.

An older person could best give this toast as the approach is serious. It could be used at the marriage of a couple who are past the first blush of youth.

Our bride and groom have today given and received a ring. This is a token that they each have given and received a great deal more. Each has given unto the other the greatest gift possible—they have given themselves. Each has entrusted to the other's hands his love, his future, his happiness, and his life. This is a flattering and shattering exchange and one which must not be undertaken lightly, nor has it. Each has given and each has received, and this exchange will continue throughout their lives.

The Good Book says, "It is more blessed to give than to receive" and this is true if the giving is free, generous and without strings. Gifts that are given selfishly for self-aggrandizement, or for bribery, or as a substitute for kindness are unworthy. Also it is more difficult to receive than it is to give. Gratitude is the sign of noble souls (Aesop). Acceptance of a great or small gift requires grace and tact and appreciation that is sincere. Havelock Ellis has said, "One can know nothing of giving aught that is worthy to give unless one also knows how to take." There must be no bookkeeping of favors granted and favors received to ascertain a balance.

> Friends must understand
> Exchange of gifts is an art.
> Give with an open hand;
> Receive with an open heart.

Carolyn and Henry are warm-hearted, generous people and can each entrust with confidence their gift of self to the other.

Ladies and gentlemen, please rise and drink a toast to the fortunate and happy couple.

EXAMPLE 19.

This is an example of how NOT to propose a Toast to the Bride. Note how the proposer—with well meant bumbling, inappropriate humor, tired stories, and lack of preparation—manages to get his foot in his mouth with every comment. Someone ought to shoot this fellow and maybe someone did. Be warned.

I sure don't know how I got stuck with this job. I've never given a speech before in my life, and boy am I nervous. You know those Spanish dancers that look over their shoulders and stomp with their heels and click those castanets? Well, that's the kind of noise my knees are making. Some people get butterflies in their stomachs—I get eagles.

I guess I'm supposed to start off with a story. I've got a real dandy. I tried it out on my wife and she said if I told it she'd leave me. That was a mighty tempting offer and I couldn't pass up an opportunity like that. So even if I'll be in the doghouse,

I'm going to tell it. This story is a real funny one—it'll kill you. I say that in giving a toast to the bride I'm like the sultan who came into his harem and looked around at all the beautiful babes and said, "I know why I'm here, but I don't know where to start." Don't you get it? He says, "I know why I'm here, but I don't know where to start." Ha! ha!

Oh, well, so much for funny stories. I tried to get out of giving this speech but I got stuck and I guess you're stuck too. Boy, am I nervous, I'm sweating like a horse.

I guess I'm supposed to say something nice about the bride. I think she looks surprisingly pretty today. It sure makes you wonder why someone didn't snap her up years ago. Her younger sister Mabel over there has already had two husbands. By the look on her face I guess I shouldn't have said that. I'm sorry, Mabel, and I'm sure all your troubles were not your fault. Ahem. Yes. Where was I? Oh, yes, about Rebecca looking pretty and I like girls to be a little—ah—I wouldn't say fat, but, ah, plump —yes, that's the word, plump, and I always thought that little bit of grey in her hair was real attractive. Though when I look close I see she's got it touched up today. Anyhow it looks real nice. I'm sure we all hope Rebecca and what's-his-name will be very happy. Lord, I've forgotten the groom's name! What is it? Oh yes, Patrick. Yes, yes. I knew it was an Irish name. Do you know why they won't let the Irish swim in Lake Michigan? Because they would leave a ring. I don't mean it, of course. I don't have any prejudices myself; some of my best friends are Irish. Anyhow I don't agree with those people who say a mixed marriage won't work. Sometimes it works just fine and as soon as the families get used to the idea, I'll bet all the hard feelings and worries and rows that have been going on backstage will be forgotten. I sure hope so.

You know one reason I forgot Patrick's name was I thought Rebecca was going to marry Sammy. They went around together for years and years and were as thick as three-day-old porridge. Sammy is that fellow down there with the pink ears.

But then Patrick came along and I guess something happened, and there goes the old ball game. You can't beat nature can you? Tough luck, Sammy. Whew, my hands are fluttering like a tambourine player's playing Flight of the Bumble-bee.

But I think Patrick is a real fine fellow—I don't care what anyone else says. It's sure nice that Rebecca's father is going to take him into the business. You know they say the best way for advancement is to marry the boss's daughter and that's just what Patrick is doing. Anyhow, I'll bet knowing how to play a bass guitar in a protest folk-singing group is real good training for a vice-presidency of a real estate company. He knows how to face the music. Ha. Ha. Seeing as how Rebecca is a little bit older, she'll probably have a stabilizing effect on him and I'll bet he does just fine. Of course Rebecca is a trained social worker and having a wife like that in a family ought to be a real asset. In fact maybe that's how she met him. Ha. Ha.

I understand we are supposed to drink a toast. Don't worry about drinking, there's hardly any liquor in it anyhow. I'm sure glad I have had such an important part in getting these kids off to a good start.

So drink a toast to the happy couple, Rebecca and Sammy—I mean Patrick—and may all their little ones be troubles.

V
Response by the Bridegroom

P to this point I have directed all my comments to the proposer of the toast. I now turn my attention to you, the bridegroom, who has been sitting there on the hot seat for what seems hours and hours.

The bridegroom always replies to the toast to the bride. Under no circumstances does the bride speak, even if the groom has fainted dead away.

If the toast is proposed to the bride, the bridegroom rises and drinks the toast with the others. If the toast is proposed to the happy couple, he does not rise or drink. The chairman will then call upon him.

Length.

Be brief. Not more than 60 seconds.

What to Say. Thank the proposer of the toast for his kind comments; thank your bride for the honor she has conferred upon you; thank her parents for entrusting her to you; thank your own parents for their help and understanding over the years; thank your friends for their kindness and good wishes (you may add a reference to the lovely gifts); you may thank your best man for his support. That is all that is necessary, but you may add a bit more. For example; invite the guests to visit you in your new home. You may refer to a comment made by the proposer of the toast and respond seriously or humorously.

Delivery. Sincerity is the keynote of our comments. You will be nervous, but do not refer to the fact and do not apologize.

Bridegrooms are supposed to be nervous and indeed the audience would be a little disappointed if you were not. The response by the bridegroom is the only speaking situation I know of where it is an advantage to be nervous, so don't worry about it. There's no necessity to be humorous. You do not wish to appear flippant and don't, for heaven's sake, say anything even faintly off-color. You needn't be solemn and may lighten your comments with gentle humor.

Speak up so you can be heard. Keep eye contact with your audience but when you refer to your bride or others look at them briefly.

An Example. Mr. Chairman, Ladies and Gentlemen (pause). It is my difficult task to reply to the toast so delightfully proposed by our friend Mr. Williams. I concur wholeheartely in his comments about Helen and we appreciate very much his good wishes for the future.

I would like first to thank Helen for the honor she has done me in becoming my wife. I think she is really taking quite a chance, but I pledge myself to do my best to live up to her faith in me.

I would like also to thank her parents for raising such a lovely daughter and for their confidence in entrusting her future to me. They may be relieved not to have me around under foot all the time and raiding their refrigerator at all hours.

May I also express my appreciation to my own parents for their love and help and understanding over many years. I know I have been a worry to them sometimes, and I know they think the smartest thing I ever did was to pursuade Helen to marry me.

I wish to thank all of you for being here, for your good wishes for our future happiness, and for your lovely gifts. I hope you will all come to visit us when we return from our honeymoon. But please don't all come at once, or you will have to sit on the floor.

Mr. Williams in his comments quoted Kipling as saying "A woman is only a woman but a good cigar is a smoke." All I can say is I'm glad I'm a non-smoker and, I would take Helen over a Corona-Corona any day.

Thank you all for your many kindnesses.